Grandmas & Grandpas

A book written
by grandchildren for
their grandparents
Edited by
Richard & Helen Exley

Published by Exley Publications Ltd.

Other titles in this series:
TO MOM
TO DAD
HAPPY BIRTHDAY! (you poor old wreck)

Published in Great Britain in 1975
by Exley Publications Ltd,
16 Chalk Hill, Watford,
Herts WD1 4BN, United Kingdom.

Second printing July 1977
Third printing November 1977
Fourth printing February 1978
Fifth printing August 1978
Sixth printing August 1980
Seventh printing September 1980
Eighth printing November 1980
Ninth printing May 1981
Tenth printing August 1981
Eleventh printing August 1982
Twelfth printing September 1983
Thirteenth printing September 1984
Fourteenth printing September 1985
Fifteenth printing July 1986
Sixteenth printing January 1988
Seventeenth printing December 1988

Copyright © Exley Publications

ISBN 1-85015-127-X

Designed by John Gorham/David Hillman
Front cover drawing by Alison Fogg, age 8
Printed and bound in Hungary.

Grandparents... fill in the gap that mothers and fathers leave out.

All the entries in this book are by real grandchildren, writing about grandmas and grandpas. They were sent in by children from eighty schools and we are deeply indebted to the teachers and children who contributed.

The idea for the book had long been in our minds, but took shape when Helen ran a "What is a grandmother?" competition in a newspaper, and was surprised how many of the entries came from children. These young people were so warm, so full of goodwill, that it seemed obvious that they should write the book.

We decided to collect more entries, and wrote to a number of schools. In all, we had close on three thousand entries, and almost every entry could have gone in. A few were badly written, or went on about grousy grandmas. But the overwhelming majority told a kind of love story; each one presented a personal little cameo, each one told of a grandparent who was precious to that child.

We had the invidious task of selecting the well-written, the well-produced and the well-painted entries: sometimes just because they had a particular turn of phrase, sometimes because they were cute, sometimes because they were profoundly moving.

We were only sorry that we couldn't squeeze more into the book, because the grandparents would have been so proud to see what the children thought of them; it would have melted their hearts.

The things the children said in their letters confirmed our belief that there is a very special bond between grandchildren and grandparents: grandparents "fill in the gap that mothers and fathers leave out", as one of the children put it.

We already knew from our work with older people that this was true. They describe in their letters the joy of a grandchild, of being able to touch and hold someone close again, perhaps years after a bereavement. People talk of a feeling of renewal in their lives, of a new meaning when a grandchild is born. And they discover that, if anything, the new grandchild is more precious even than their own firstborn. They now have time to enjoy the relationship, to get close to a child, and really to give.

And now these entries from the children give the other half of the story. They show that this love is returned in full. It isn't a one-way thing.

At first the child doesn't seem to be aware of much more than the chocolates and the presents. Many of the entries from the younger children make grandma seem like a walking ice cream factory, a fount of goodies and Christmas presents. But very soon, especially amongst the girls, something else emerges. They begin to appreciate the time a grandparent has to give. Many of the letters talked of grandma or granny "as a best friend", somebody who you could talk to about your boyfriend, somebody you could say things to that you couldn't tell your parents.

It isn't that parents lack understanding; but within the family situation there may just be too many pressures. And in big classes at school, the teachers may not have much time either. Adults just don't seem to be there, ready to listen; and if a grandparent has managed to keep the channels of communication open, this is when they reap the reward of a close and lasting relationship.

Editing the book has been immensely enjoyable. It has proved, for us, that the relationship between the generations is alive and well. It's not dead, as sociologists would have us believe when they talk about the breakdown of the extended family and grandparents living in isolation.

In a way, this book is a way of saying thank you to grandparents; it's a way of saying thank you for all the Band-aids on sore knees, all those apple pies, all those patient readings of well-loved stories, all the lessons, all the time so freely given. One little boy perhaps summed up the feeling of most of the entries when he wrote simply: "I send my love to grandparents, all over the world."

Richard & Helen Exley

A grandma is old on the outside and young on the inside.

John Wright Age 7½

Granpas are delightful things they date back to the last century.

Simon Welch Age 10

grandmother

Lynn

grandfather john

Lynne

Grandmothers and Grandfathers give a home a friendly touch.

Marco Orlandini Age 9

My christening gown was made from her pre-war wedding dress. History for me is memories for them, yet they are not aged or dusty: Grandma and Grandpa are real. A whole part of my childhood would be missing if I had not known them. With them I am at once a little girl and an object of pride and hope for the future. *E J Slessenger*

Happy or sad I think that grandmothers are the wisest, most understanding people in the world (excluding of course grandfathers). *Jane Moore*

Catherine Jones Age 10

Definitions

A grandfather is the one who helps you with your homework, even when he doesn't know how to do it.

Gary

Your grandad is the one that tries to make you tough. But when you try to be tought, you get beat up.

Bradley Simpson Age 12

A Grandmother is a lady who either sleeps or knits.

Sara Spurrier Age 12

A Grandmother corrects your grammar and wipes immaginary dirt from your cheeks.

K Phillips Age 11½

Grandmothers are people who still do the spring cleaning.

Maureen Dracey

She's the person who tells me all the things about my parents, they would rather not have me know.

Sarah Scott Age 15

My Grandpa is tough outside, but soft hearted inside.

Justin Birch Age 10

Grandparents are cheerful, sentimental old things.

Donna Pearce Age 12

Andrew Age 9

The dictionary says, quite simply, a grandmother is "a father's or mother's mother" but had there been room, I'm sure they would have added...
Grandmothers are

Generous giving people
Regular churchgoers
Afternoon snoozers
Never (well, hardly ever) irritated by you
Drinkers of whisky and water
Members of a ladies' church group
Owners of old jalopies
Crossword fanatics
Hospitable hostesses
Eaters of brocolli, spinach, cabbage and beans
Relaters of gossip
Scrabble players

and without Grandmothers, the world would be a different place.

H. Bulley

Mark Marvis Age 9

A Grandmother is kind and doesn't like all the new coins and other small change—she gives us them quite happily. *Bobby Marston*

A Grandmother doesn't criticize. *Anne Joplin Age 11½*

Grams's always have something up their sleeve like gum drops. *Gemma Cummings Age 10*

Grandmothers wander around and look very suspicious. Grandmothers' bones are old. *Caroline Curtis Age 11*

Helen Alsop Age 8

Justine Strachan. 7 yrs old
My Grandmother is my mammys
mother She is verey old and
nice as well and she brings
me nice things my Grandfather
is my mommys father a
Grandmother is a verey old
lady my mommy is my
Grandmother dauter and my
Grandfather dauter as well
She lives at 79 Chirton
Rd

Justin Strachan Age 7

My Grandmother is a knitting machine.

Carolynn Shaw Age 7

A Grandma is a very, very, very, very nice person.
My Grandma is my best Friend.

Terry Worthington Age 9

A Grandmother never tells us lies.

James Denness Age 10

My English grandmother is always prim and
proper. She always keeps her house neat and tidy.
Whenever I say "Lounge" My grandmother
corrects me saying "Drawing Room, my dear".

Teresa Age 10

My Grandma looks so nice and old,
With her crinkled up face,
And her squashed up nose
With her ten year old glasses
And her long silver hair,
She looks as if she was bought at the antique fair.

Winston Age 12

There is one thing that bothers me it is my gran
hadly ever gose out because she is to old to go on
the back of the moter bike.

Lenny Age 9

Candy Age 6

12

A GRAND MOTHER

Simon Steer Age 11

13

Mostly sympathetic

A Grandmother is an elderly person who watches people walk past and hopes that someone will come and visit them. *Simon Martindale Age 10*

My Great Grandad has a habit of buying me chocolates and then eating them. *Jay Coquillon Age 11*

When some granmas shake hands with you they leave some money in your hand. *David Shipton Age 9*

Grandmothers always come up with advice, which is given whether you need it or not. *Rita Bourke*

A Grandmother is a little old lady, who comments on the weather and how tall you are getting, tells everyone the latest gossip and all about her son who came to see her. She lets you do what you shouldn't and if mom complains she says "Remember when you were little and I caught you dipping your finger in the sugar bowl? You're not too old to get your ears boxed". *Jackie Thompson*

Grandmothers are the old in the world of the young, and are continually having the "good old days" wiped out of the conversation. They long to help and yearn to be loved. *Rita Bourke*

A Granny is jolly and when she laughs a warmness spreads over you. *J Hawksley Age 11*

Her shoes are all old fashioned now and her bloomers wow o wow. *Sandra Fowler Age 9½*

14

Appearance

My Grandmother is crumpled.

Richard Humphrey

Some grandmothers are very small and some grandmothers are very big. You can get all different sized grandmothers, you know. *Andrew Deboata Age 8*

The thing that makes grandmas so jolly looking is the fact that as they get older they grow out instead of up. *Jacqueline Hope*

My Grandmother is not very tall, but come to think of it she is not very short either. *Sarah Green Age 10*

My Grandma is a little fat but Nowa-days most Grandmas are. *Alan Richards Age 9*

Mine looks funny. She has got a long face and her chin wobbels when she walks. *Michael Barbridge Age 7.*

A grandmothers clothes remind me of a Princesses clothes, they are pretty and soft. *Catherine Cardwell Age 9*

A grandmother can be tall or small but mine is midium and cuddly fat. *Catherine Cardwell Age 9*

Grandmothers used to be formal, strict, old fashioned and covered in slippery black dresses tinkling with jet trinkets and smell of mothballs. My father's mother is a grandmother but she is comfortable and warm and soft, scented with cologne and baking.

E J Slessenger

As you have proberly noticed my granny thinks time stands still and wears the same clothes as when she was small (except a few sizes bigger).

Paul Milsom Age 10

Grandmothers wear quite long coats to cover up their knobbly knees.

Carol Stacey Age 7

A Grandmother tells you to put on a coat or you will catch a cold. A Grandmother fusses over you. A Grandmother wears old fashioned clothes.

Angela Mutch Age 11

This is my grandwa

Aligon

Allison

Sandra Dale Age 9

Habits

Grandmothers are sort of a pest. They want everything so spick and span and neat. *Caroline Webb Age 10*

Grandmothers some times lock the door when they come out and when they get to the garden gate they go back to make sure they have. *Eunice Hopkins Age 10*

Grandmothers are fat and put wigs on before they go to the door. *Richard Dunmow Age 8*

My Grandma has a good habbit of eating cake every evening. I like this because I have some too. *Nicholas Dunne Age 11*

My Gram has a habbit of naming things she calles her freezer Fredda and her two radios big willy and little willy. *Allison Anthony Age 10*

When my mother gets thirsty she has a cup of tea but when my granma gets thirsty she has a gin and tonic. *Jackie Holleley Age 10*

My Grandma has some very extraordinary habbitts. *David Heys Age 10*

Perhaps the best definition of the grandmother, is somebody who spent her time telling your mother what not to do, when she was young. And now spends her time, criticism your mother for giving you the same advice. *Calvin Giles Age 12*

Mine knits all the time, though we have socks for more than 10 years. *Anette Bromner Age 14*

Jacqueline Hollely Age

She's got oblong eyes because she watches television all day.

Sandra Rendell Age 10

Now she needs me

My grandmother is a box of
childrens building blocks
Each a different size and shade
Each one different from the other.

When I was young and cut my knee
She would become an enfolding, purple curve of
                                  sympathy.

If I was caught doing, any wrong thing
She would be a rectangle, dark blue glowing.

If in dire need of help am I
She is a pulsating orange pillar,
That touches the sky.

When something special I have
Into a bouncing restless globe, she will go
Of a beautiful sunflower yellow.

To the dismal depths of depression I have been
So she has become a pyramid of gentle green.

When she is ill
And I make her jovial
A blazing turquoise star,
tells me I'm her cheering up pill.

Funny, and strange, how time should change.
Amazing how time should beg
I needed her once now she needs me.

Quentin Radford Age 11

22

The nice thing about her, is that she says that I've got two homes, my home and their home.

Julia Gambold Age 9

Brigid Cooper Age 7

23

grndfather
pain

Emilio Esteban Age 10

25

Grandpas

My GrandDad can fix nearly everything. *Helen Age 9*

Grandpa is usauly the grumpest of the pair. He is kind but not as kind as your nana. *Elspeth Bridges*

Grandads are very lazy and sit back smoking and watch old westerns. Some grandads stay asleep all day until they feel hungry then they wake up. After supper they go back to sleep. My Grandad calls me ham bonse. *Mark Ward Age 9*

My Grandfather is a funny sort of character because every time I go down to his house to borrow somthing for my Mother he says "No" and then lets me borrow it. *Colin McRae Age 11*

My Grandad pretends he has a jelly bean tree. *William Sholl Age 8*

Grandpas always have a bag of tasty goodies in their pockets well as lots of junk and odds and ends, such as a penknife, string, a compass, an animal bone and a toy soldier. *Fiona Gibbings*

Grandfathers like cabbage and caulieflower and other awful things. *Beth Age 10*

My Grandad is a safety shield against an angry mom. *Rebecca Smith Age 11*

My grandpa used to rough and tumble with my brother But now both of them are past it. *Richard Thompson Age 12*

Inflation
Inflation they say
not like the
good old days.

Catherine Ashley Age 9

Andrew Barnett Age 10

My grandmommy loves my granddad and my granddad loves my grandmommy. Sometimes they get mad at each other and they fight. I feel bad. When they get lovey dovey again and kiss I feel good.

Kimberly Age 5

Grandparents are for helping with homework, teaching you about sports and world policies and playing games with you. Of course grandads tell 'quiet down', 'hush', 'behave', but I love my grandad and gram and I guess I won't trade them in.

Rosa Age 10

Julian Humphrey Age 10

My Grandparents.

I would like my Grandparents to be very loving, generous and thoughtful. I would like to be very kind in a way that they would care. They would make me stay with them for as long as I could, and they would give me money to spend, without fail, every time I would go to their cottage. They would let me do what I wanted to in their enormous garden, which had stacks of things to do in it. Climbing trees, jumping walls, chasing rabbits and lots of other exiting things. Somtimes Grandad would tell me stories of old-fashioned times. He would also play games with me which he would play when he was young. The two of them would never forget lots of presents for my birthday and for Christmas. They would always know what was right for me.

My Grandad would be short and stout, with a long curly mastchs, coloured grey-white. He would have a little bit of white curly hair, just around the sides. He would wear very smart looking clothes.

Geoffrey Baker   Aged 10 ys

29

Grumblers & grumps

My Grandma is always saying don't touch, put that book away don't read in bed or something like that. She sayse put that car away. pick that up don't drew in that reading book. and at bedtime she even does it more. Go to sleep or you will be late for school in the morning, be quite, don't play with that, don't rip the blankets and then its brechfast time dreedfull don't lick your dish, brush your teeth wash your hands. I'm glad when I get to school and I don't hurry home. when I get home she starts again. did you get some stares yes Grandma. How many? Five. not good enough. and at bed time she starsts again. *Dawn Age 7*

Some days when we've been there two long they should be called a new names Grumppa and Groanie. *Alberto Fernandez Age 8*

My grandmas always yakking
My grandads a real pain
Between them
They make quite a pair. *Susan Nicoll Age 11*

My Fathers Mother is rather grumpy she likes to watch the news and moans to us when she hears about bombs as if we had planted them. *Allison Anthony Age 10*

Grandmoms are awkward and they never want to do what other pepull are doing. *David Hoggarth Age 9*

Some people may think grandma's are special. I don't think grandma's are special they are just relatives.

Steven Alan Jones Age 8

Diane Barnett Age 7

Grannies used to be old with grey hair. But nowadays grannies can be quite young.

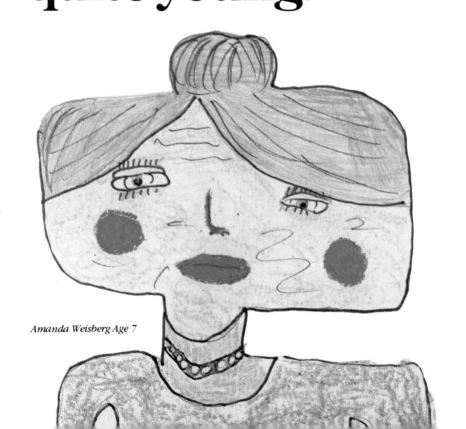

Amanda Weisberg Age 7

About age

Grandmas say that the title makes them feel old—like a Grand piano, I suppose. As an alternative, how about Supermom?

Isobel Blaber Age 14

My Grampa looks very old to me and my brother.

Trevor Cox

My Grandparent's are both conciderate. They are both about the same age but that doesn't seem to bother them.

Elizabeth Rose

A Grandma is very nice and is some-time's old.

Lynne J Gregory Age 9½

My grandmother is getting older than she thinks.

Clive Owen Age 10

Grandpa is over 40 and under 90.

Alexander Hambly Age 10

Grammas always act young and seem young but are old.

Lucy Deamer

They aren't young, But my dad's catching up.

N Arthur Age 13

When they tell my parents Not to be childish I feel very, very young.

Peter Wilson Age 12

When she is sitting by herself she looks old and lonely. But when she has company she looks young again.

Mary O'Gorman Age 11

I Thought Dad was rather old—untill I met grandpa.

Ian Laing Age 13

my grandpa and grandma love each other because they hold hands and he keeps telling her silver threads among the gold.

Sarah Anderson, Age 8

Ryan Age 9

A fascination with teeth

My Grandma has special toothpaste and pretending teeth.
Clive Smith Age 7

Once she lost her teeth later when I was running the bath they floated to the top. I think she is very typical.
S Enright

They often have a few false teeth Which in the morning are often found out Which lie besides the bed which are quite frightening They look like elephants fangs.
Helen Turner

If theres one thing that annoys me about her is, she clicks her false teeth and she does it when theres any music going keeping in time with the tune.
Alison Brice

My Grand Mother is very unusual.
She has a very funny face.
Shes got silver hair and only four teeth left.
I fink she should have two teeth out that will leave two.
David Fitzgibbon Age 7

My Grandma has false teeth I do not like the look of her when she's got them out.
Richard Morrey Age 8

I thing my Grand-dads great, he stayed with us all Christmas. He has no teeth and he hasn't got faulse teeth. When my Grand-dad laughs I can see the top of his gums and it makes me laugh to.
Janette Wright

My grandma hates false teeth. She is scared her
dinner will get stuck underneath. *Steven Whiskin Age 8*

"Will you look at that" shouted Grandpa and
took out his false teeth and shook them at the
driver who had just passed us. (Grandpa does not
like being passed he hardly ever is though because
he drives at such a speed). When we came up
behind him, Grandpa waved his false teeth and
shouted "You crazy old fool". *D Farnworth*

24 January.

My Grandma
My Gran cannot sleep,
So she gets up very early.
When she goes upstairs
No one helps her, or seems to care.
My gran wears false teeth
She takes them out when we have tea.

My Gran is very old
And is very, very bold
She is very kind
And for her age, has a very good mind.

Michael Croker Age 9

37

Food and cooking

She cooks delishush diners. *Michael Barbridge Age 7*

Nans are people who give you cream and waffles and watery orange drink and expects you to eat it all. *Susan Garmston*

My grandmother makes lots of cakes, but the nicest thing about that is she lets me put the decorations on the top. *Tanya Burch Age 9½*

Grandmothers fruit cakes are more fruit than cake mixture. *Jane Hitchcock*

She makes real gateau and cake which never fall flat like my mothers. *Sarah Richardson Age 10½*

My Grandmother is a good cook. Choklitikake is my best feest when I go to stay. *Mark Harris Age 9*

A faint aroma of gingerbread and all good things mixed together, seems to linger all around a grandmother. *Elspeth Gordon Age 12*

Rachel Williams

Reginald

The best thing that I like about my
Grandmother is, when she gets up in the morning
and the heater's on she'll come and get dressed
there. She'll stand by the heater and warm her
behind and then my grandpa will come along and
he stands there looking at me and then he looks at
Grandma and he then gives a funny laugh, then
creeps up to her and he rubs her fat tummy
"Reginald" she shouts.
Her face then glows and wrinkles up and her eyes
are full of laughter, her cheeks are a pair of roses
and her glasses fall on to her nose.
"Reginald", she shouts, "if you don't stop that I'll
have a burn't behind.

Beverly Ward

Militant Grannies

They appear on the strikers camp, with rolling pins
All armed to the teeth,
All ready to do battle with gnashing teeth,
One granny lets go with her Fiery left hook,
Which lands a union leader in the pond,
Where he floats on his back, like a dead duck,
They swing out left and right
With all their might,
And strike down every enemy in their sight,
And as the strikers Flee the scene.
Then the grannies take up the chase,
They swing their handbags like a mace
They smash them down, one by one,
And as each one Falls,
All the grannies let out their victory calls.

Adrian John Bradley 12 years 9 mths

Sarah Woolston Age 9

Katy Osborne Age 8

Grandpas

A grandad is a person you never forget, never.
I'm proud that he's my grandad.
And I'll never forget his hand in mine as we walk
down the street together.
Suzanne Cairns Age 13

I think my grandpa is fantastic, most grandpas
are. If you are saving up for something they are like
walking piggy banks and give you money.
Jeremy Shilling

I love the magic Grandad does, especially the
peppermints he makes appear from my ear!
Rebecca Smith Age 11

Grandpa grows great rasberries and always
pretends not to notice us eating them.
Tracey Knight Age 8

He cares for everything,
Everything,
But himself.
Joanna Read Age 12

My Grandfather always falls to sleep after the
football results are over, and he wakes up when he
hears his buzz word "food".
Stephen Mouncher Age 11

My grandfather is not really like any old man,
for he is 86 years old and has a special driving
license and swims in ice cold lakes in which I
would never dare to put my foot. A person must
not think of him as a first class madman, or at least
a person can think as a person wants but I still
think and will think he is the nicest and most
considerate person I have had to bump into.
P Ham Age 13

A grandfather is somebody who outbalds Kojak.

Nicholas

Samantha Weinstein Age 9

Belinda Sacks Age 9

My Grandma and Grandpa

AARON. WATSON

Grandmas and Grandpas are very kind to you. But sometimes they keep you talking when you're in a rush to leave. But they can't help it I suppose. have two grandads and one grandma. My other grandma in heaven but she was always helping other people so I know she is a very special angel.

Sharon Watson Age 9

Your Granny loves you. No matter what you do.

Paul Myers Age 10

I have thought it out that the youngest a legal grandmother can be is thirty three and three quarters. This is not often the case. Normally they are in their late fifties or early sixties. To a young child, this seems ancient, but as they grow up, and watch their parents pushing the forties, they see how young they really are!

I always associate grandmothers with knitting and darning—very useful when you go through your socks at the rate I do! They are often widows and therefore have to be visited fairly often. If they drive, they are highly lethal—either driving too slowly or in the middle of the road (or both!) If and when they send you postcards from their seaside resort (where they go and visit great aunty Flo) their writing is always thin, wobbly, spidery and totally illegible. They feel the cold far too easily, require an electric blanket, thermal underwear, wooly long johns and the heat on in the middle of summer! Their cutlery is normally silver (whether they can afford it or not) and the table cloths and napkins are always stiffly starched.

They love potted plants, radio, television and old china ware. They have an annoying habit of never having their "spectacles" handy when they need them.

One big problem they all have in common is being very deaf. This means that everyone has to speak slowly and loudly for them to hear. When given a hearing aid for a Christmas present they complain when you speak too loud!

At meal times even though they eat very little, they feel obliged to leave something (an old fashioned habit I believe) which is very annoying indeed.

On the whole despite their annoying ways, I like grandmothers very much, knowing that someday I'll probably end up like them!

L Horne Age 13

Linda McLaughlin Age 9

All the time in the world

She has a part of her own and a future which belongs to everyone. She leads an empty life of her own which is filled by the lives of others. Most of all she is a person who will always have time to see you when the rest of the world is busy. *Gill Webb*

Grandmas are always slow but they do not mind for they have all the time in the world.
Malcolm Andrew Age 10

Grandmas and Grandpas have nothing to do But talk to you. *Catherine Mellors*

Grandmothers are dearly loved by every-one. When your mother tells you you are going to spend a day or two at your grams you can't wait. When you fall over and cut yourself your parents are always too busy to put a Band Aid on. So the only person who is not too busy is gram. At night time they tuck you into bed and make you nice and snug. *Jane Hibbs Age 9*

A Grandmother is a person who will never get tired of your chatter no matter how long you go on for. *Julia Macdonald-Smith Age 12*

I personally believe that grandmas would knit to the end of the world! *Simon W. Debenham Age 11*

My Grandmother is very patient. She would have to be with me around! *Helena Leeson Age 10*

Grandparents live in their own funny world where time seems To go backwards. *Kevin J Brown Age 12*

Paul Yeowell Age 10

Bribery

It's very noisy in our house and when Grandma comes over she says, If you can be quiet I'll give you some spending money. And we are quiet then for a little while.
Joe Cassidy Age 12

Grandmas are very necessary for letting you do things you are not allowed to do generally, like watching "The Late Night Horror Movie" or eating too many waffles than are good for you, or not making you eat carrots.
Kate Clancy Age 14

My granny lets me lick the cake mixture when she is finished. She lets me leave my food, and she spoils me so much that when I grow up I won't want anything.
Sandra Webb Age 10

Most grandmothers will spoil you if they can, but parents will butt in just as you're about to eat your third helping of cake, it's awfully annoying.
Helen Schwendener Age 11

The 'grandmother' is usually a great source of the children's income as she nearly always gives them quite a lot of money after a happy but exhausting visit. The money is usually for all her grand-children ("little angels"). They usually stick their hands out suggestively or start whining that they can't afford a teddy bear or a skiing trip.
Charles Robert Fenwick Linfoot Age 13

Every time I went over to her house I got some more money. As I liked my grandmother I went over to her house about five times a week.
Andrew Austin Age 10

Dad says you're spoiling us but do they listen oh no. Presents here presents there presents everywhere. I like Grandmothers spoiling me. Darlings they always say, while Dad, thinks what rubbish.

Catherine Ashley Age 9

One of a grandmother's most prized privileges is to spoil her grandchildren. She arrives armed with pockets full of goodies, and special pocket-money to buy the child the things denied it by its parents for numerous good reasons — no cheesecakes because they have too much sugar for example. Granny stuffs the child full of ice cream and cakes, and then leaves before it is sick.

Tessa Ing

When my mother tells me to do something I do not want to do I tell my Grandmother and she talks my old lady out of it.

Sonia Allan Age 10

My Granma lets us stay up and watch horror films. My Granma is really really really nice.

Mark Robinson Age 9

Colin Fleetham Age 11

This is my Grandmother

Her frail body carries her along
Slowly but surely she crosses the road
It seems miles long
As she makes sure of her steps.
This is my grandmother
The kindest of her kind.
Looking back I remember the things she did for us.
When we were young we stayed with her
We had fun together
The walks, the talks, the games
When we were ill she spent a lot of time looking
after us
Even when there were things to be done
We were her sole concern always.
Now we look after her.
Talk to her and look after her with her ills
We try to pay her back for her kindness to us
But it would take forever.

Susan Punter

Who can measure Grandmothers?

She seemed in a mask or costume
As much as a hat or glove.
For in her talk was youth and life
As pure as a beautiful dove.

Her mask was of wrinkled skin
Attached onto her face.
It was not really her because it did not fit
It belonged to another time and place.
But the more she talked and as I watched her
She shed the mask from her face.

A light as new as spring shone in her eyes
And in her movements a youthful grace.

Age is but a word of time
A thing which we created.
A thing which is measured like the bleeps on a
radio.
But who can measure grandmothers
And put them into hours and minutes
Of knowledge kindness love and care?

The nearest measurement there is for me
Is that They are like the jewels in a watch
The watch is the world
And the wheels are the tools of the spring
The spring is life
The more jewels the better the watch.
My Grandmother is no diagem or paste
But a clear and sparkling diamond.

A Grandmother

This small pale woman, a mother grown old,
By her hair and her wrinkles her age can be told,
Her past is a dream, an impossible hope,
For her children are married now and able to cope.
Her role as a mother has vanished and gone,
As the moon loses its role when up come the sun.

But the birth of a Grandchild means new life has
begun.
The birth of a Grandmother, Parents and son.
Now there is a role, a part to be played
For this small pale woman, a grandmother is made.
New qualities of joy have begun to show
Is this the same woman whom I used to know?

She now is a grandmother, a person who shares
A person who loves and a person who cares,
Her face has an expression of understanding and
love,
Of normal standards she towers above.
Her time to all is so generously given,
A person who I'm sure is destined for heaven.

Sally Lloyd Jones Age 14

Cindy Age 8

56

My Grandmother is a refuge. She is a gentle 'relic' of the past (although I don't thing she would like me calling her that). She is part of the past it is nice to think she has journeyed through the years and is still so sensible and kind.
They take care of us, in loving us, but ask for nothing in return.

Susan Philpot

Tracy Chennelles Age 9

How can she make them understand?

She sits there living,
In her memories,
The young men, the laughter
The river boats,
Summer picnics and romance,
Romance unlike any other,
Special, strong and
Everlasting.

Nothing is left now,
Only memories,
Though life goes on, but
She cannot understand
Remembering her long quiet childhood,
Which no longer remains,
Life was simple,
And days were long and happy
Children now are so restless
And unloving, taking everything
For granted, awaiting their maturity
Wasting their long, lazy days
Of innocence
Oh, how can she make them understand?

Susan Legg Age 15

Diane Barnett Age 7

A Refuge

When you go to her with your pride bruised
and hurt; she never takes sides, but helps you to
think fairly and to see the other person's point of
view. She knows the problems that all the
members of her family go through, and is able,
from her own experience to give advice.
She is usually a sympathetic listener — to what
must seem to her, your personal inconsequential
(compared with some of the ones that she has to
face during her life-time) problems. She never tries
to advise her children on grand-children, unless
she is asked to do so, and lives her own life, far
enough away, so as not to be a nuisance, but close
enough (to her children) to be a help in a crisis. In
short a grandmother is a refuge.

Amanda Evans

Yesterday

She's called "Nana" and she tells tales that she
told to mother when she was a child. Many stories
of exciting adventures that happened a long time
ago. They did not have the luxuries that we have,
but waltzing in their large living room when the
furniture was pushed aside, singing round the
piano, telling stories by the blazing fire whilst they
ate hot muffins. Skating on the frozen lake in
winter, riding in a steam train, all these more than
make up for television and trips abroad. I hope my
Nana will stay with me for a long time, and when I
have the farm I long for, she will be able to live
with me and feed the chickens. We will have a
blazing log fire and she will tell us stories of the
past.

Dawn Williams Age 10

Love

I would not want my grandma to go up to heaven.

Michael Orloff

My Grandmother is not plump but nice and comfortable, when she sits you on her knee you can nestle down and feel safe and secure.

Angela Dobson Age 10

We call her Nanny. She is not very old
I don't mind how old she is.
I would not want another nanny because ours is the nicest one.
I wouldn't swop her for any sum of money.

Jane Clarke Age 10

My grandma is in heaven but she was always helping other people so I know she is a very special angel.

Sharon Watson Age 9

Grandmothers are very useful for showing you how to do lots of different stitches.

Caroline Webb

If I have a secret I will always tell Grandmother not anyone else.

Joanna Simmonds Age 8

You can tell them secrets of all the bad things you have done and they won't tell our mothers. Then they tell you about all the wicked things they did when they were little.

If we get bored with our mother and father telling us what to do, there's always someone waiting for us with her arms out.

Helen Tidy Age 9

A Grandmother is a mother who has a second chance.

Caroline Flitcroft Age 11

A grandmother is someone you love helping.

Jane Farrell Age 11

Kim Curd Age 11

Grandpas

LEE COX

Caroline
Hurst 7¾

A grandpa is someone you can take advantage of. A grandpa is someone who let's you go under the sprinkler. A grandpa is someone who always loses in the fight with grandma. A grandad is great.
Kelly Age 8

Happiness for me is eating pizzas, for grandpa it's snoring.
Pedro Age 9

A grandfather is the only one who can call me "gimpy" without hurting my feelings.
Miles Age 10

Darrell Age 10

Sarah Age 10

(speech bubble) come back be- for dark

A grandpa is someone who tells corny jokes, and then expects you to laugh.

Elena Guttierez Age 13

A grandpa is the person who helps you eat your food when you can't eat it all, so it looks like you at it all.

Farrah Age 10

A granddad is someone to buy you a new skateboard and try it out and almost ruin it and break a leg when he thinks he can ride it perfectly after a few lessons.

Dan Age 11